Student Workbook for The One and Only Ivan

By:

John Pennington

Cover by Pixabay.com

The lessons on demand series is designed to provide ready to use resources for novel study. In this book you will find key vocabulary, student organizer pages, and assessments. This guide is the Student Workbook. The Teachers Guide will have answers and an open layout of the activities. The Student Workbook can be used alone but it will not include answers.

Look for bound print <u>Teacher Editions</u> on Amazon.com

PDF versions can be found on Teacherspayteachers.com

NAME:

TEACHER:

Date:

Vocabulary Box

Definition:

Draw:

Patient

Related words:

Use in a sentence:

Definition:

Draw:

Imagination

Related words:

Use in a sentence:

Vocabulary Box

Definition:

Draw:

Ponder

Related words:

Use in a sentence:

Definition:

Draw:

Canopy

Related words:

Use in a sentence:

NAME:

TEACHER:

Date:

Vocabulary Box

Definition:

Draw:

Precision

Related words:

Use in a sentence:

Definition:

Draw:

Crevices

Related words:

Use in a sentence:

Vocabulary Box

Definition:

Draw:

Unadorned

Related words:

Use in a sentence:

Definition:

Draw:

Undaunted

Related words:

Use in a sentence:

NAME:

TEACHER:

Date:

Vocabulary Box

Definition:

Draw:

Parasites

Related words:

Use in a sentence:

Definition:

Draw:

Digestion

Related words:

Use in a sentence:

Vocabulary Box

Definition:

Draw:

Migrate

Related words:

Use in a sentence:

Definition:

Draw:

Forage

Related words:

Use in a sentence:

Check Your Reading

Question: Who owns the animals?

Answer:

Question: What is the name of their home?

Answer:

Question: What is wrong with Stella?

Answer:

Question: What does Ivan and Julia have in common?

Answer:

Assignment: Interpret the meaning of "It is never to late to be what you might have been." - George Eliot. How do you think it will show up in the story?

Character Sketch

Ivan

Personality/ Distinguishing marks

Draw a picture

Connections to other characters

Important Actions

NAME:

TEACHER:

Date:

Character Sketch

Stella

Personality/ Distinguishing marks

Draw a picture

Connections to other characters

Important Actions

NAME:

TEACHER:

Date:

Research connections

Source (URL, Book, Magazine, Interview)

What am I researching?

Pablo Picasso

Facts I found that could be useful or notes

1.

2.

3.

4.

5.

6.

Compare and Contrast

Venn Diagram

Three Visitors

My Visitors Return

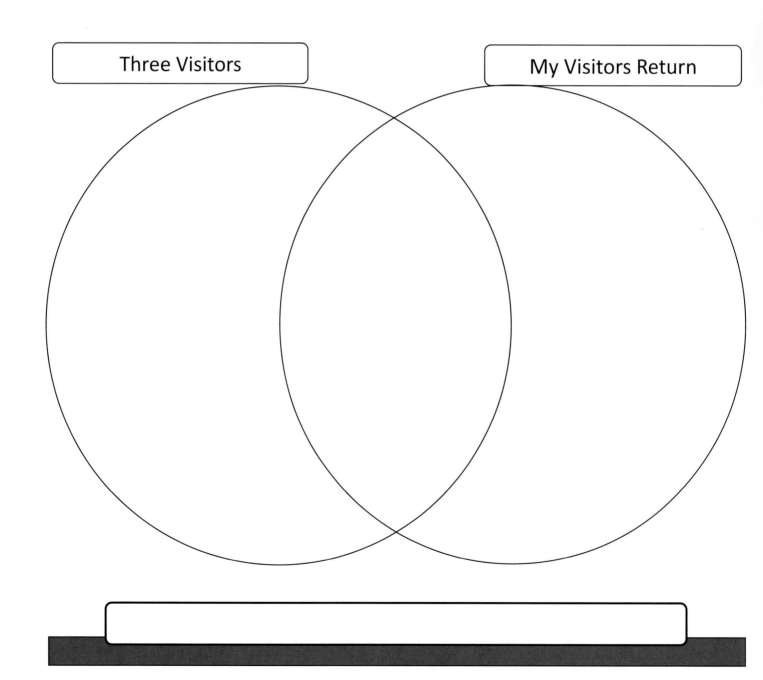

NAME:

TEACHER:

Date:

Draw the Scene: What five things have you included in the scene?

1   2   3

4   5

Vocabulary Box

Definition:

Draw:

Domain

Related words:

Use in a sentence:

Definition:

Draw:

Harmonica

Related words:

Use in a sentence:

Vocabulary Box

Definition:

Draw:

Amends

Related words:

Use in a sentence:

Definition:

Draw:

Dignified

Related words:

Use in a sentence:

Vocabulary Box

Definition:

Draw:

Heritage

Related words:

Use in a sentence:

Definition:

Draw:

Opportunity

Related words:

Use in a sentence:

NAME:

TEACHER:

Date:

Vocabulary Box

Definition:

Draw:

Responsibility

Related words:

Use in a sentence:

Definition:

Draw:

Emphasize

Related words:

Use in a sentence:

Vocabulary Box

Definition:

Draw:

Contemplating

Related words:

Use in a sentence:

Definition:

Draw:

Mesmerized

Related words:

Use in a sentence:

NAME:

TEACHER:

Date:

Vocabulary Box

Definition:

Draw:

Unpredictable

Related words:

Use in a sentence:

Definition:

Draw:

Addled

Related words:

Use in a sentence:

Check Your Reading

Question: What does Ivan find to draw with his black crayon?

Answer:

Question: Who is the new arrival to the Big Top Mall?

Answer:

Question: What does Ivan promise Stella?

Answer:

Question: What happens to Stella?

Answer:

NAME:

TEACHER:

Date:

Assignment: Design the perfect habitat for an animal (your choice of animal). It must include a minimum of five features designed specifically for the animals benefit.

NAME:

TEACHER:

Date:

Character Sketch

Mack

Personality/ Distinguishing marks

Draw a picture

Connections to other characters

Important Actions

Character Sketch

Ruby

Personality/ Distinguishing marks

Draw a picture

Connections to other characters

Important Actions

NAME:

TEACHER:

Date:

Research connections

Source (URL, Book, Magazine, Interview)

What am I researching?

A Circus

Facts I found that could be useful or notes

1.

2.

3.

4.

5.

6.

NAME:

TEACHER:

Date:

Lost Scene: Write a scene that takes place between Ivan and Stella , Bob, or Julia

Advertisement: Draw an advertisement for The Big Top Mall and Video Arcade

NAME:

TEACHER:

Date:

Vocabulary Box

Definition:

Draw:

Nimble

Related words:

Use in a sentence:

Definition:

Draw:

Tolerant

Related words:

Use in a sentence:

Vocabulary Box

Definition:

Draw:

Venture

Related words:

Use in a sentence:

Definition:

Draw:

Revenge

Related words:

Use in a sentence:

Vocabulary Box

Definition:

Draw:

Temperamental

Related words:

Use in a sentence:

Definition:

Draw:

Trudge

Related words:

Use in a sentence:

Check Your Reading

Question: What is the name of Ivan's sister?

Answer:

Question: Ivan stops using the word domain and begins using _____?

Answer:

Question: Where does Ivan decide Ruby needs to go for her safety?

Answer:

Question: Why is it difficult to read Ivan's painting?

Answer:

NAME:

TEACHER:

Date:

Assignment: Drawn an picture on 16 sheets of paper like Ivan. Shuffle the stack and give to another person. How much time does it take for them to understand the picture? Record how long it takes for several people if you have time.

Character Sketch

Bob

Personality/ Distinguishing marks

Draw a picture

Connections to other characters

Important Actions

NAME:

TEACHER:

Date:

Character Sketch

George

Personality/ Distinguishing marks

Draw a picture

Connections to other characters

Important Actions

NAME:

TEACHER:

Date:

Research connections

Source (URL, Book, Magazine, Interview)

What am I researching?

Africa

Facts I found that could be useful or notes

1.

2.

3.

4.

5.

6.

NAME:

TEACHER:

Date:

Precognition Sheet

Who ?

What's going to happen?

What will be the result?

Who ?

What's going to happen?

What will be the result?

Who ?

What's going to happen?

What will be the result?

Who ?

What's going to happen?

What will be the result?

How many did you get correct?

NAME: _____

TEACHER: _____

Date: _____

What would you do?

Character: _____

What did they do?

Example from text:

What would you do?

Why would that be better?

Character: _____

What did they do?

Example from text:

What would you do?

Why would that be better?

Character: _____

What did they do?

Example from text:

What would you do?

Why would that be better?

Vocabulary Box

Definition:

Draw:

Suspiciously

Related words:

Use in a sentence:

Definition:

Draw:

Impossible

Related words:

Use in a sentence:

Vocabulary Box

Definition:

Draw:

Curious

Related words:

Use in a sentence:

Definition:

Draw:

Distinguished

Related words:

Use in a sentence:

NAME:

TEACHER:

Date:

Vocabulary Box

Definition:

Draw:

Patient

Related words:

Use in a sentence:

Definition:

Draw:

Protest

Related words:

Use in a sentence:

Vocabulary Box

Definition:

Draw:

Inspect

Related words:

Use in a sentence:

Definition:

Draw:

Property

Related words:

Use in a sentence:

NAME:

TEACHER:

Date:

Vocabulary Box

Definition:

Draw:

Associate

Related words:

Use in a sentence:

Definition:

Draw:

Lumber

Related words:

Use in a sentence:

Vocabulary Box

Definition:

Draw:

Loam

Related words:

Use in a sentence:

Definition:

Draw:

Juvenile

Related words:

Use in a sentence:

Check Your Reading

Question: Who pushed for a change of habitat for all the animals at the Mall?

Answer:

Question: How did they try and get the animals into cages?

Answer:

Question: What happened to Ivan and Ruby?

Answer:

Question: What happened to Bob?

Answer:

NAME:

TEACHER:

Date:

Assignment: Research and defend the value of a Zoo. Are they good places for animals? Why should we have or not have them.

NAME:

TEACHER:

Date:

Character Sketch

Maya

Personality/ Distinguishing marks

Draw a picture

Connections to other characters

Important Actions

NAME:

TEACHER:

Date:

Character Sketch

Kinyani

Personality/ Distinguishing marks

Draw a picture

Connections to other characters

Important Actions

NAME:

TEACHER:

Date:

Create the Test

Question:

Answer:

Question:

Answer:

Question:

Answer:

Question:

Answer:

Top Ten List

1.

2.

3.

4.

5.

6.

7.

8.

9.

10.

NAME:

TEACHER:

Date:

Sequencing or timeline

1.

2.

3.

4.

5.

NAME:

TEACHER:

Date:

Advertisement: Draw an advertisement for _____

Chapter to Poem

Assignment: Select 20 words found in the chapter to create a poem where each line is 3 words long.

Title:

_____ _____ _____

_____ _____ _____

_____ _____ _____

_____ _____ _____

_____ _____ _____

Character Sketch

Name

Personality/ Distinguishing marks

Draw a picture

Connections to other characters

Important Actions

NAME:

TEACHER:

Date:

Comic Strip

Compare and Contrast

Venn Diagram

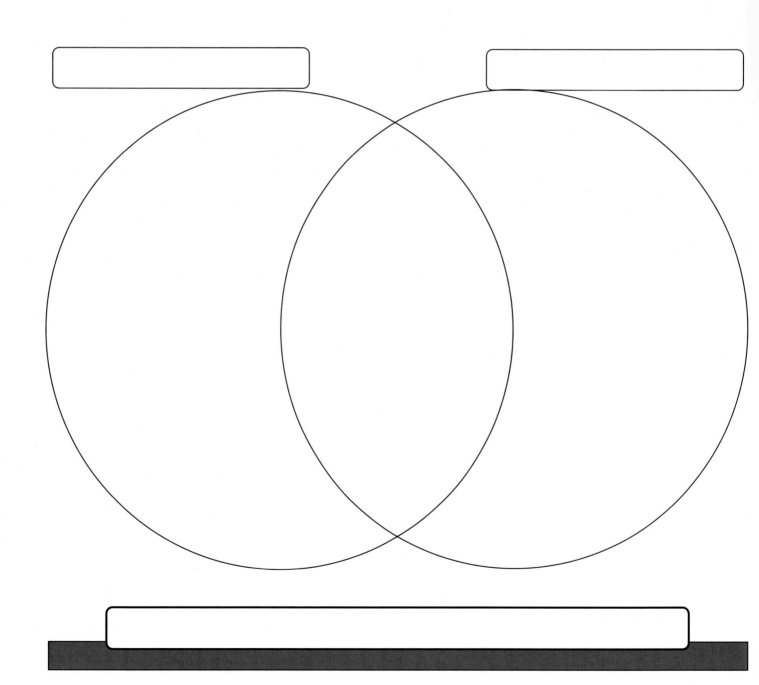

NAME:

Create the Test

Question:

Answer:

Question:

Answer:

Question:

Answer:

Question:

Answer:

NAME:

TEACHER:

Date:

Draw the Scene: What five things have you included in the scene?

1   2   3

4   5

NAME:

TEACHER:

Date:

Interview: Who _____

Question:

Answer:

Question:

Answer:

Question:

Answer:

Question:

Answer:

Lost Scene: Write a scene that takes place between _____ and

_____

NAME:

TEACHER:

Date:

Making Connections

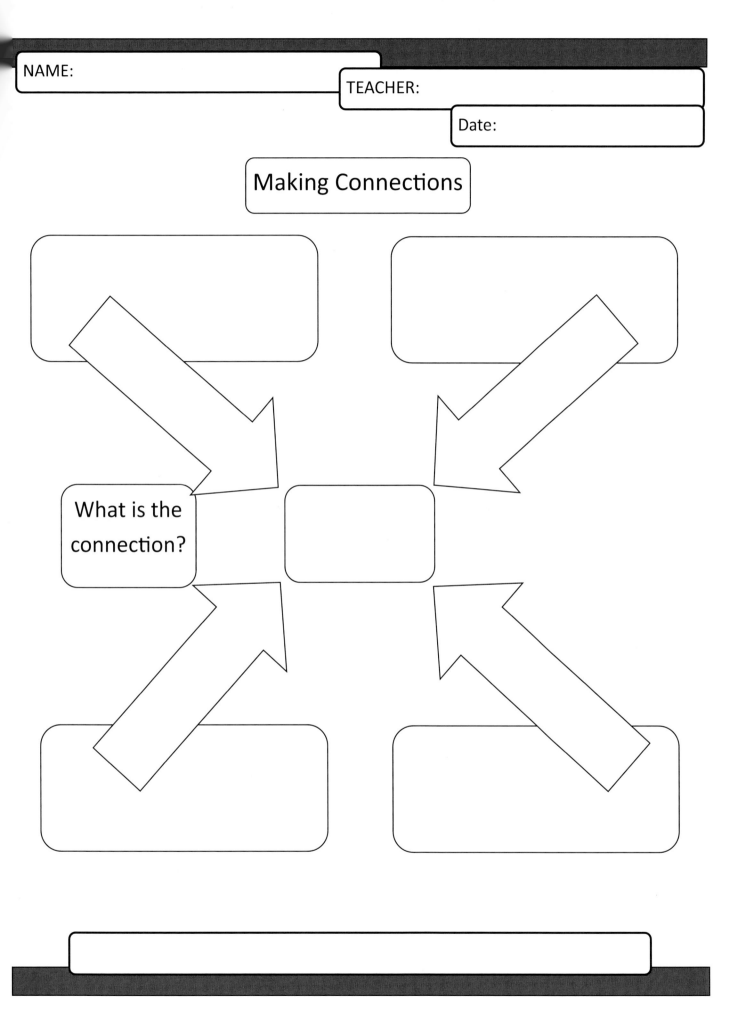

What is the connection?

NAME:

TEACHER:

Date:

Precognition Sheet

Who ?

What's going to happen?

What will be the result?

Who ?

What's going to happen?

What will be the result?

Who ?

What's going to happen?

What will be the result?

Who ?

What's going to happen?

What will be the result?

How many did you get correct?

NAME:

TEACHER:

Date:

Assignment: Pyramid

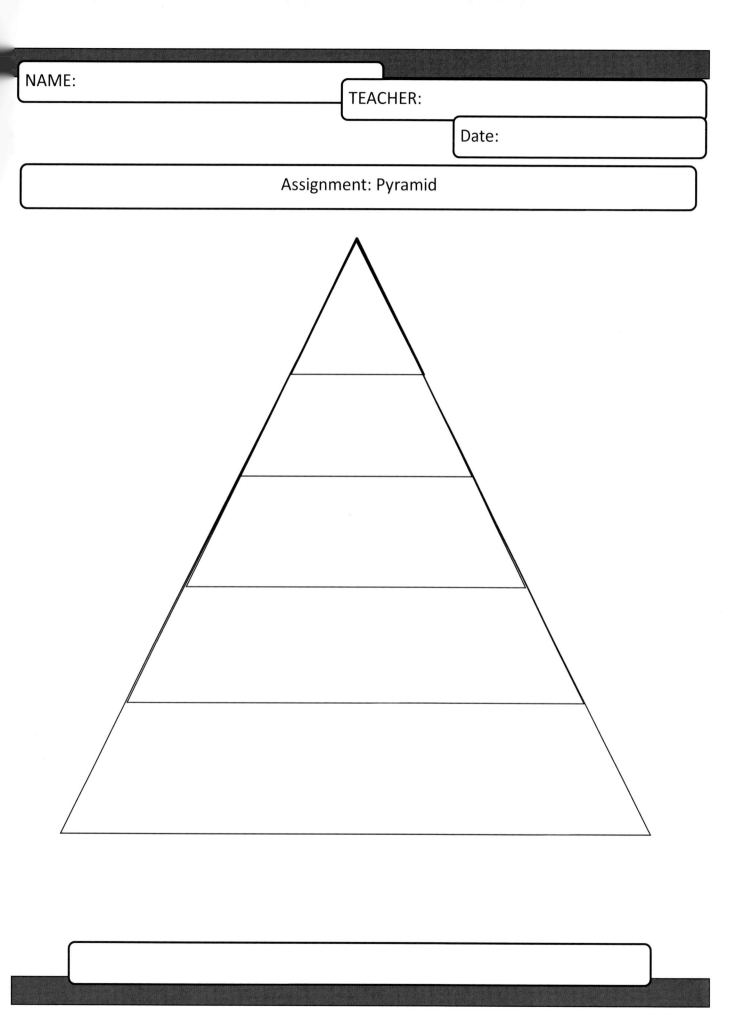

NAME:

TEACHER:

Date:

Research connections

Source (URL, Book, Magazine, Interview)

What am I researching?

Facts I found that could be useful or notes

1.

2.

3.

4.

5.

6.

NAME:

TEACHER:

Date:

Sequencing or timeline

1.

2.

3.

4.

5.

NAME:

TEACHER:

Date:

Support This!

Supporting text

What page?

Supporting text

What page?

Central idea or statement

_____

Supporting text

What page?

Supporting text

What page?

NAME:

TEACHER:

Date:

Travel Brochure

Why should you visit?

What are you going to see?

Map

Special Events

NAME:

TEACHER:

Date:

Top Ten List

1.

2.

3.

4.

5.

6.

7.

8.

9.

10.

NAME:

TEACHER:

Date:

Vocabulary Box

Definition:

Draw:

Word:

Related words:

Use in a sentence:

Definition:

Draw:

Word:

Related words:

Use in a sentence:

NAME:

TEACHER:

Date:

What would you do?

Character: _____

What did they do?

Example from text:

What would you do?

Why would that be better?

Character: _____

What did they do?

Example from text:

What would you do?

Why would that be better?

Character: _____

What did they do?

Example from text:

What would you do?

Why would that be better?

NAME:

TEACHER:

Date:

Who, What, When, Where, and How

Who

What

Where

When

How

NAME:

TEACHER:

Date:

Write a letter

To:

From:

NAME:

TEACHER:

Date:

Assignment:

NAME:

TEACHER:

Date:

Add a Character

Who is the new character?

What reason does the new character have for being there?

Write a dialog between the new character and characters currently in the scene.

You dialog must be 6 lines or more, and can occur in the beginning, middle or end of the scene.

NAME:

TEACHER:

Date:

Costume Design

Draw a costume for one the characters in the scene.

Why do you believe this character should have a costume like this?

NAME:

TEACHER:

Date:

Props Needed

Prop:

What text from the scene supports this?

Prop:

What text from the scene supports this?

Prop:

What text from the scene supports this?

NAME:

TEACHER:

Date:

Soundtrack!

Song:

Why should this song be used?

Song:

Why should this song be used?

Song:

Why should this song be used?

NAME:

TEACHER:

Date:

Stage Directions

List who is moving, how they are moving and use text from the dialog to determine when they move.

Who:

How:

When:

Who:

How:

When:

Who:

How:

When:

NAME:

TEACHER:

Poetry Analysis

Date:

Name of Poem:

Subject:

Text Support:

Plot:

Text Support:

Theme:

Text Support:

Setting:

Text Support:

Tone:

Text Support:

Important Words and Phrases:

Why are these words and phrases important:

Made in United States
North Haven, CT
29 October 2024